What is Love?

Written by Isabel Gravely

Illustrated by Valerie Bouthyette

What is Love?

©2023 Isabel Gravely
No part of this book may be reproduced, stored in a retrieval system, or transmitted by any means, electronic, mechanical, photocopying, recording or otherwise, without written permission from the author.

Requests for speaking events, extra book copies or permissions should be addressed to: isabel.gravely@gmail.com

Printed in the United States of America

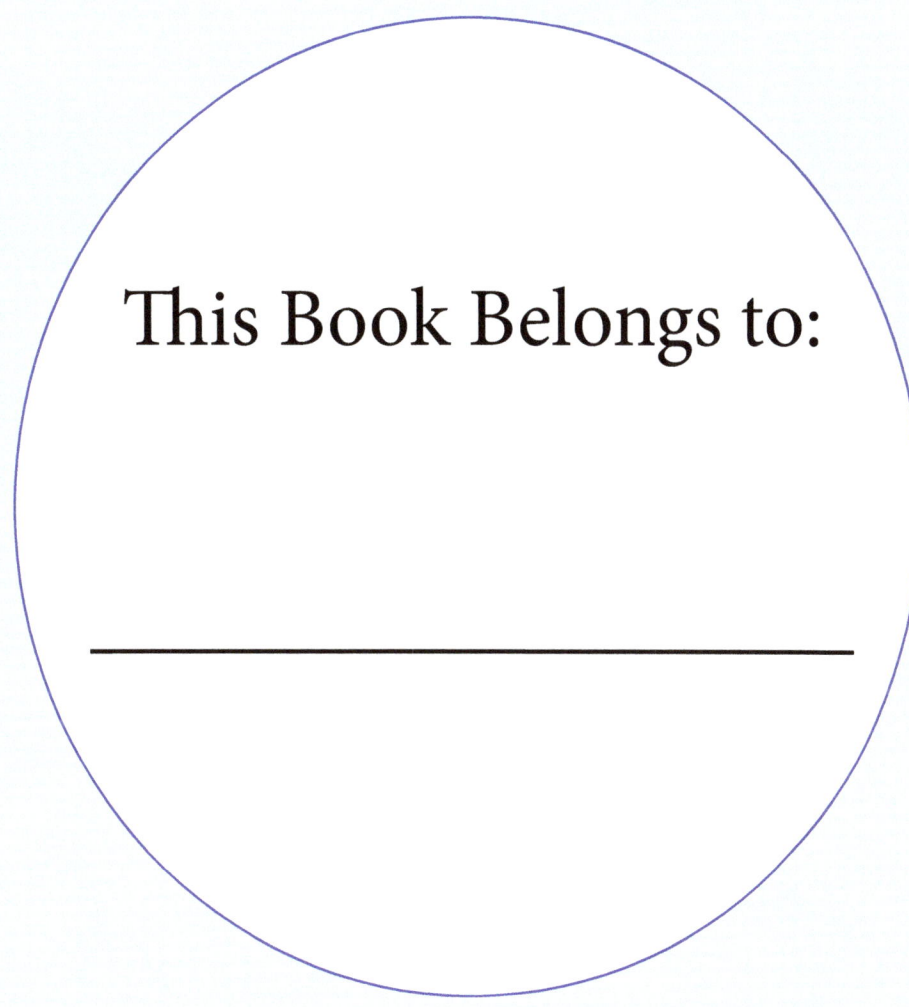

This Book Belongs to:

_____

Love is when dad
reads me a bedtime story.

Love is when my brother teaches me to play soccer.

Love is when
my sister plays the violin
to make me smile.

Love is when
we all dance in the kitchen
while mom and dad cook.

Love is when I get sick
and mom and dad take care of me.

Love is when my family shows patience with me when I throw a tantrum.

Love is when
I talk on the phone
with my grandma.

Love is when
I play with my cousins.

Love is when my aunt and uncle spoil me with gifts.

Love is when my grandparents give me dessert.

Love is when
all my family gets together
and is thankful
because we have each other.

Love is my family and me!

www.ingramcontent.com/pod-product-compliance
Lightning Source LLC
Chambersburg PA
CBHW061353010526
44107CB00011B/916